# DUAL

*poems*

# DUAL

## MATTHEW
## MINICUCCI

ACRE

CINCINNATI 2023

Acre Books is made possible by the support of the Robert and Adele Schiff Foundation and the Department of English at the University of Cincinnati.

ISBN-13 (pbk) 978-1-946724-67-0
ISBN-13 (ebook) 978-1-946724-68-7

Designed by Barbara Neely Bourgoyne
Cover art: Zoran Borojevic on Unsplash

The press is based at the University of Cincinnati, Department of English, Arts & Sciences Hall, Room 248, PO Box 210069, Cincinnati, OH, 45221-0069.

Acre Books books may be purchased at a discount for educational use. For information please email business@acre-books.com.

# CONTENTS

## Confessions

## Nouns [that should not be] in the Dual

In addition to languages where either all nouns or no nouns have a dual, there are those where only some nouns have, or are most likely to avail themselves of, this category. According to Humboldt, if only some nouns have a dual, it will always be those denoting "objects which in nature occur in pairs." Such natural pairs are for example the twin body-parts and sense-organs, the two great heavenly bodies taking turns at illuminating the earth . . . opposites in terms of kin relations, the partners in commercial transactions, [and] the twin constituent parts of various artifacts.

—Frans Plank, "On Humboldt on the Dual"

In a field
I am the absence
of field.
This is
always the case.

—Mark Strand, "Keeping Things Whole"

# DUAL

# A

Consider the dual. As in: the obsolete number. As in: the *not singular* and *not plural* of things.

**Examples:**

ὄσσε—χὲιρος—Ποδός.

Translation: *eyes—hands—feet.*

This is the way we once considered two things inexorably connected. Not to be confused with duel, D-U-E-L

often confused with duel, D-U-E-L.

**Related Moment:**

Achilles realizes Patroclus is dead.

**Additional Related Moment:**

Achilles realizes it's his fault.

**Results:**

The flames, the actual flames, that consume his head as he storms through the Trojan lines.

**Examples:**

ἄπυρος.

Translation: *untouched by fire.*

**Conclusion:**

Incorrect usage. Everyone is touched by fire.

# B

Consider the choice. For example: the impulse to forget your father's face.

**Explanation:**

Masculine patronymics. As in: the noun plus *ia-das, i-das, a-das,* or *ion.*

**Example:**

Achilles = πελίδες.

Translation: *son of Peleus.*

**Concept:**

The boy who would be king.

**Further Examples:**

The other boy whose name means *glory of the father*

πατρο plus κλέος.

**Reality:**

The boy who died in your arms; your actual bronzed armor and weapons.

**Consequences:**

The importance of tense.

The pluperfect: βεβήκει.

Translation: *he was gone.*

**Observation:**

The stars that night.

**Conclusion:**

What you thought you had all the time in the world to see.

# Γ

Consider the question.

**Example:**

*What if?*

**Explanation:**

This is in the dependent subjunctive [mood].

**Further Examples:**

The *if happily*, the *in the hope that*, the *on the chance that* [mood].

The optative, the potential optative, the dependent potential optative [mood].

**Problems:**

What is the difference between the subjunctive and optative?

See: J. B. Sewall, Bowdoin College, *On the Distinctions Between the Subjunctive and Optative in Greek Conditional Sentences,* American Philological Association, 1896.

**Abstract:**

Only vivid presentation, that is: supposed fact *contingent* on X, as opposed to supposed fact *as merely conceived* by X.

**Further Examples:**

An expression exclaimed with present or aorist infinitive:

εἰ κεν θάνατον γε φύγοιμεν.

Translation: *if we should escape death.*

**Conclusion:**

These are the moods of impossible wishes.

# THIRTEEN WAYS

## OF LOOKING WEST

## Thirty-Seven Thousand Feet above Illinois

Calm is a kind
      of impossibility. You see

the buck isn't some
      sort of gambler's luck, it pulls

                    at the seams, means

nothing but hum to the rattle

                    sleeping next to you; blue, before
                    the bounding deer below. Slow and snow

and I miss the powder

                    that covers
                    every piece of the Midwest

                          in winter. There's less
                          now, where I call home

a plow shudders in below, scrapes
      at a pitch I can't know           glides like dusk or rose
                    garden rows, moves the way

                    a fountain pen
                    breaks its own nose

                        just to say anything
                        at all.

## Reading Eliot on a Boat in Elliott Bay, WA

sound, so they say,

this observer that taps or laps

engine's twin: forced air, there's history

hear: a ring and bright flag; snow

stuck in the riprap. No notes

on rocks, only water. Water

then light. Light

is a farewell; wave's distant Doppler,

like a driver, almost lost; snaps a rudder,

there, abaft the speaker, I can't

crow to you like sea lions smiling, song

along the lighthouse here. Nothing

then mountains. Mountains

then darkness, darkness,

then

## Walking the Flood of Fire Trail in Kimberly, OR

what does green sound like? Grief,
you never did hear the doxology; in Greek, always
more fragile than you could know. So, there's
the missing mountain. Once, there was something;
to see: me, sliding across the sand
for the rattle, listen for the sun, look at it:
"like another world," but it's this one,
lost in this timid tortoise shell. Here,

under glass perhaps. Dear, but
dusted, bronze bream, always
an end in the bend beneath the wall beneath
a body encased in smoke, broke for you
like a snake waking to greet the day. Watch
this book built in painted panes. You say it's
*over so soon, kiln of the moon*, lot tossed and
there are three voices: you, me, & some

impossible sea: celadon, sweet in the smoky mute

## Looking for Salmon in the Wilson River at Tillamook State Forest, OR

It runs, rabbit, static to
a stake left grounded; static, again,
what rocks might lie beneath this brief break
when water expels from the mouth
bubbles from grammar school
blood. I'm hearing the fast, the new grass
never sung without instruments. Footsteps
of oncoming time. It all sounds the same
lye, and by and by
chinook to push forward like brief silver line

a river in more than just bend or break
station to station and you've left to see
I can't blame you. I'm much the same way
just out of the lungs it sounds like
water fountain; rusty; filled with holy
wind pushing along some song
perhaps, trying to stay out of this path
but that's a lie. The truth is:
some other mouth opens. It isn't time for
red. There's a single rock crashing instead

which doubles

again;

becomes, like all things,

more of itself

## Considering a Wooden Bridge at Latourell Falls, OR

Once, we found a cold mantle of sound swept
        from shoulders to ground in a valley where rocks sing

                                            wounds, mostly; some mortal
                                            was the first to hear. This place

where you say *cold* or *stay*, or that someone once prayed
        to this might, just a light April spray that

                                            cuts whole rivers from the mountain, like
                                            whey. Or the last remains of a day, lost

beneath scratch-climb fingernails; dark star ablaut
        grout in the dog-bark mud, all bespoke of a particular

                                            nothing; so pounding an end is water. But
                                            I haven't mentioned the river log, the ears'

pitch-pine gravity where voices cross; moss
        and cost in each binary day. If night, say *something lost*; if

                                            fog, say *path is warning's din*; or *hollow sin.*
                                            Say *swept* and *white bristles walk*; at least

here the sun can't win, and so
        once again, all of this begins.

## Watching *Julius Caesar* at the Oregon Shakespeare Festival in Ashland, OR

it's not what you see. A sea, it seems
like a river; light where the lark
over foam that roams and all
nothing to you. A bone: a bucket of loam
the stage shook like a knife sheathed above
that could be nothing & yet so cold;
but with brief clasp of hands. A wave to me

lies here: misattribution, some mistake, the sound
makes his mark. An actor, a player shouting
this talk of Rome means
that was important, once, how a bird called to
quiet knees we do not fall upon. A night, longing
and yet with bold heart did Caesar go
to be, for a moment, unheard; the whole day yet

not a single word escapes the din undrowned

## Waiting at Champs Barbershop in St. Johns, OR

piano's keys, teeth in the gear & everything
I may, if pressed, say sharp or flat lost to
some field. Nothing left to yield under
the weather's calling for more rain, maybe hail
and farewell to the man with three months to live,
a last middle C, my hands before the sea's
retaining wall. Nothing at all. No sand here

shackles like riff; repeated. Rainy day and
a windrow decade caught in
this horn's wail, or wall, or water we bail
to accompany the barbershop sermon: quick
scene in the wonder about why he never returned to
broken bones that split a bit of this heart's
caught in the round wheel of another day where

the barber says "It's all well; hell, I don't even remember the sun"

## Picking Up Trash on the Docks of Cathedral Park, OR

listen: the spider-weld green moss
season spoils. Flute mic, stones' dice that
arbor or harbor, though
that is a Homeric Greek joke
fingerprints point in silt soiled,
lingering spot of every mottled
gloss. Hear another gear near
what goes into those staccato
impossible boulders, or felled tree

clay day of another rainy
portent of a possible new scar
it all depends on breath and yes
this broke on some black river wake
north by sight, and we right the lost
former water bottle pocked with lipstick's
smoky engine darkness & we fear
soft cut chords that finger some
hull, nearly silent in the nothing-day blues

## Listening for Bird Species in Lady Bird Johnson Grove, CA

it's a brass class of penny whistles
on branches, the black oystercatcher
picked bark; hole struck in a plastic lid
burnt by butane; melted, stinging
missiles marking territory, terror's
a truck right through the bass of
trees. Turn down the sound. Talk stars
along the sidewalk that hangs in the fog;

I guess, what I'm trying to say is: today
sounds the same as every other
tinnitus day: tincture of fear, a tin
prick flap that can't be uncoiled from the
flag mast. Sometimes, at night, I can hear
the clear-sound snap of stern
& I begin to cry. There you are:
there you are again

## Escaping Sneaker Waves at Big Lagoon, CA

what a difference
an ocean makes,
like some sleeper
aloft in flee. It's me
who shouldn't be here
it's sinking shellfish
wax's wane; pane of glass
that moves before it makes
it's a pool-cue pond
in the eardrum: portent
this passion left suffering
in the grass; missed mass;

that the wide sea is me;
I can't explain it.
this Sitka spruce, is
only shutters. Shouts at the tree
genuflected at the knee; knots
in blue-black morning:
pearl trapped against the transparent
there's a fool in this storm
maybe it's elk, or artillery; laughter
or that leap from land's-end
like anything else alluvial: it builds,
it breaks. Interred at last

## Tourists Touching Honu in Punaluʻu, HI

belief might be nothing more than
rush grass against rock,
a wall, a wail, lava welds that pool
waves like a father's hands delivering a
metaphor. It's just empty space beneath
pebbles in the curve of a palm; it's
tossed into the back of every posed picture
painted like childhood's chalkboard; midnight

black sand beach, or some charge from bull
or rock from nothing at all. Less than
a tincture, push some sound
frame filled with no picture at all. It isn't
the dark pumice of pined rock; pewter like
basalt monolith, another green turtle
hawksbill lagoon; the ocean's just-empty room
in June; no color at all like tonight's empty moon

# A Love Poem with Coquí in the Rainforests of Volcano, HI

Frog, or fog, or the brief motion that begs

    a log from some fallen tree.             Listen:

        like Sunday's terse mass           it rains more in the past,

    think about it:                 here we sit and

stitch our sails while barn cats prowl in pronation       there are

                                    all kinds of song.

    I haven't the heart to tell you:

        the one made of lehua and rain;

                                    the one

                                        where a twisted tree follows

    a marriage proposal, just like       Daphne's fall. Imagine:

nēnē in the night sky; soft          call, graze or browse

    though it doesn't matter; there are seeds

                                    in the shrubs, shouts

        from a broken house mouse       left sordid by the door, nothing more,

     'Ohi'a grows everywhere          you say, even lava

that's just cooled. Listen to that laze-glow night:

                      it sounds

            ash-breath hue;

    hip-click coquí call

           leading me back home to you.

## Sheltering from a Sudden Storm at the Níʻaulani Rainforest in Volcano, HI

'Ohi'a lehua; two hundred years, smooth as pebbles
on some hidden porch, guardian of some
old birds in a new concrete world cracked by the
forest unfurling; or wehe; smooth to rough-hewn
voice, and voice again. Pocks, a plague on both
stages, assuaged by vertical volcanic forms, which
reach for the heavens, but usually stay here with us
like some basalt sculpted by floorboards. Lava
changes you: its flow; its low slung gun slowly
unbuttoned like a knock at the forest door
nothing more. False whistle; deep dirt kick like mud
flung light.

      Come in.

beneath numinous & silent birds. I dream of an 'apapane
sea you'll never see again. Let koa sleep; all the
arguments of our fathers. Yours is about guava; old,
so I can't hear the rain, again. You admonish me with
*rains about to begin,* or just did, so wind
pins back behind the ears. So wet, let this wash
without any sort of moon, or moon, or moon; soon,
we'll hover above. It sounds like love, but it
hung down like some perfect bark gown
have I told you how 'ohi'a can grow down, fall and
tomorrow wash away? What may you see in the far
Flung light?

      Come in.

# AJAX, UT

.

## WILLIAM AJAX UNDER[bullet]ROUND STORE*

*The unique two-story underground building was established in 1870.*

There's red inside the hills.
Like veins. Rivulets, in
the rills. Here, there is red

everywhere. I don't know
what it is. A tree? No.
Blood? If so, it's far away.

*Shortly thereafter a post office called [bullet] was added.*

In Tooele, you are
greeted by *Get Some Guns*
*& Ammo.* Of course, I

don't know exactly why
you would need an indoor
range when you have nothing

but space behind you here.
Two M16 weapons
crossed like swords, or M4s,

maybe. I don't really
know. Laughs in quotes, it says
"get some," in ~~blood bright~~ [bullet] red.

*The building was [bullet] x 100 feet, in some [bullet] the lower floor was 20 feet below ground.*

White-brick, old broken-down
movie theater called The
Ritz, ~~complete~~ [bullet] with beauty

parlor right next door. Also
broken down. Who has set
foot there in ~~sixty~~ [bullet] years?


*The excavation was done by William Ajax using a [bullet] shovel and wheelbarrow.*


The red: it's trees, changing
~~colors~~ [bullet]. It's fall here. Still
far away, but it's fall.


*The [bullet]'s support timbers were cut from juniper and pine trees.*


There is a Tooele ~~Army~~ [bullet]
depot here: disused trucks;
a detention center.


*[bullet] trees were located in the mountains west of here where he walked to and from each day to [bullet] the timbers.*


Detention center over-
looks this entire ~~mountain~~ [bullet]
valley heading south on

Route 36. Can you
imagine? Every day
you look out & you see

the one giant ~~windmill~~ [bullet]
in this huge wide-open
space you could do any-

thing with if you could just
      get away.


*The roof was constructed of poles covered with juniper boughs, sod and clay.*


They mine gravel here, it
seems. Something else perhaps but
this is not a quarry.


*The [bullet] was [bullet] by sunlight coming through the south-facing windows in [bullet] roof.*


~~Stockton~~ [bullet], now, and the first
thing that greets you is *speed*
*zone:* 40 miles an hour;

a church, at least it looks
like a church, but ~~empty~~ [bullet]
now; just ~~empty~~ [bullet] parking lot.


*Shoppers were offered a wide variety of merchandise, food, clothing, housewares, hardware, tools
and medicines.*


Stockton appears to be
one road, maybe five or six
streets. There's a bar here called

Miners and a Sinclair
with a dinosaur on
the sign, as if telling

you where the oil came
from. Whose blood it is that
pumps through the veins of your car.

*Goods were arranged in a department store style.*

Outside of Stockton, this
is the west. Broken down
fences, all of which need

mending. One long thread of
,power lines moving from
the town into desert.

Here: a valley completely
surrounded by mountains.
The land itself scrub, short

bushes, dry grass. Sort of
like prairie but without
some plant I can't recall.

*It was estimated the value of the merchandise was in excess of $70,000.*

In the middle of no-
where two old dump trucks sit
stem to stern, front to back

pressed against each other
like a yin-yang symbol,
or the 69. Doors

are open but no one's
there. I have no idea
how long it's been since some-
                one was there.

*Patrons came from the mining camps, sheep and cattle ranches and the communities of Rush and Vernon Valley.*

For a Mormon valley,
there's a whole lot of what
appears to be power

lines strung along the rail-
road. Iconography.
Incredible. These huge

towers, monuments, arms
outstretched every fifty yards.
Sacrifice in each one.


*Meals and lodging for travelers was provided.*


Outside of Ajax, I'm
in public lands, all of
them run by Bureau of Land Management.


*Their livestock was also cared for in sheds and corrals located west of the present highway.*


This spot looks like it's an
abandoned cow pasture.
There's the loading chute. Old

fences. A mountain range
in the background. I can't
begin to describe it.


*Wild grass-hay was cut in [bullet] meadows.*


The William Ajax store,
underground but covered
in [bullet] holes. People

and their target practice
for years. There's a train in
the distance, cut across

the valley, looks like a
cargo train. To my left,
Bud Light cans everywhere.


*It was sold to miners in Stockton, Ophir and [bullet].*


All that remains of Will
and Emma Hughes Ajax's
store are the ~~mounds~~ [bullet] of dirt
            just east of the monument.


*The coming of the railroad through Rush Valley made supplies and travel more accessible, thus*
*ending much of the need for a store in [bullet].*


Stapled to the fence is
a sign that says "private
property, no ~~trespass-~~ [bullet]

ing," and I'm not inclined
to disagree. There are pants
hanging on a cow fence.


*William Ajax dies in 1899; his family operated the store until [bullet] when they liquidated the*
*merchandise.*


~~Broken~~ [bullet] glass everywhere.
Based on the beer cans, this
spot is still being used

*The building was abandoned, and later it was [bullet] (perhaps [bullet] transients camping at the building).*

by transients. ~~Resume~~ [bullet]
driving down the Pony
Express Trail ~~Mountain~~ [bullet]

range to the left, hills to
the right. Still desert, still
scrubland.

*All that remains are [bullet] mounds of dirt just east of the monument.*

Note: Land for sale on Route
36, ~~unclear~~ [bullet] mile:
call a guy named Mike, he's
         where the pavement ends.

*All italicized portions are quoted directly from the Utah Historical Marker currently standing at the original store site. [bullet] has been added to denote unreadable portions scarred by gunfire.

# NEW DRAFTS
## OF CERTAIN STORIES

## On Men Talking about ~~Euripides's~~ Seneca's *Trojan Women*

O, what a fearful sight—was Hecuba;
The Greeks had found her crouching in dear tombs,
The very tombs where all her sons lay buried.
And there she clung: she tried to kiss their bones.
    —*The Metamorphoses,* translated by Horace Gregory

When the lightning bolt came probing
that tree of the conversations,
he who was struck by it raged about injustice.
    —Rosario Castellanos


When John threw Astyanax off the roof of Eastgate Tower,

the baby fell as everything else does:


accelerating to a predetermined speed,

decelerating to a sudden stop—


I wasn't there, but I'm told Hecuba *wept bitterly,*

Andromache stood stoic, unmoved, her face white:

once great city *reduced to ashes.*


Weeks later, John recounted the story to me.

There was no mention of the baby, only

a slight push, mimed, as if against the air itself,


the barely discernible street vendor below, screaming

about hot dogs or pretzels.


John spoke about a cat he had as a child,

hit by a car, and how when he found her that morning

the left and right paws were still grasping at the air.

He curled his lips back into his mouth; turned

slightly and mumbled something about a new job

in Watertown, network management,

that Eileen had gone to stay with her mother

for a few weeks, maybe more.

"All I can tell you," he said getting up to leave,

"is that *weeping eases troubles,* & that this hurts me

more than you can possibly understand."

## Hero and Leander

I guess the Hellespont looked much the same
when from a drowning girl it took its name.
And Helle's death insured its infamy.
With such a record, is there hope for me?
   —*The Metamorphoses*, translated by Horace Gregory

Whoever loved that loved not at first sight?
   —Christopher Marlowe

It always took two things, light and will: / when Hero's light went out, Leander's will washed away

his last thoughts were of her, then water, then darkness / her last thoughts were of him, then

night sky, then stone or earth

The Hellespont is 38 miles wide

The Hellespont is now called the Dardanelles

Forgive me, Hero, my arms are no longer strong as oars (fisherman are right to fear

my nightly journey) / they are right to fall in love closer to home

In 1598, Christopher Marlowe did not mention their deaths / this is called a comedy

all energy moves from localized to spread out; Orpheus, for example / was torn to pieces

by maenads because he had abandoned Dionysus; was torn to pieces

because he had abandoned all love since Eurydice

Orpheus's lyre was taken by the gods and placed in the stars / his soul was taken
down & placed in Hades / this is the farthest apart they had ever been

Phaethon driving his father's horses through a cold, barren
sky / and losing his grip / the daughters of Helios mourning

their brother / the bark they grew to try and stop the pain

I have seen tears slow as amber

Antigone and her father wandered the desert / it was the only place without judgment

Echo, whose gossip cursed her to forever repeat and / never create, still speaks: / anemic,
frail, suspect / an echo, a complaint, faded letters from the desert

Hero is victim to sleep and wind: lights, for lack of a specific term, eventually go out

Leander is victim to direction and exhaustion: sometimes the one thing keeping us
steady fades away; arms, mythological though they are, give up

It is possible when Hero's light went out, Leander finally / lifted his eyes above the tower
in the distance. It is possible he might have seen

a star he never knew existed.

## Agamemnon Farms in Homer, IL

My prize was conquest; may it never fail again.
  —*Agamemnon*, translated by Richmond Lattimore

His grief that like a shadow walks
        Beneath the beast at noon,
Makes him like a god, and talks
        Of comfort late or soon.
  —Peter Russell


It's harvest here by the side of the road:

brittle corn and *Glykys apios,* sweetly named.


The field has been plowed three times, dark

gold and black earth left to capsize the caterpillar,

the earworm, and the aphid.


A single sheep is lost in the pasture,

but the bull provides no consolation.


The wool runs red.


Agamemnon stretches out his arm and points to each part of the combine.

That night, to no one, he claims to own the sky.


In the morning, he pulls what's left from the ground,

with spade and axe and fingernails.

"All of this was ocean," Agamemnon says, "and the mouth of the world

drowned in salt."


"Now, we've filled the hole with brittle gold, forgotten

*the great stream of the sea,* & the sharp of the shark's tooth."

## That I carried the *Aeneid* in my pocket for a semester

Poor boy, when Fortune came with happiness,
was she so envious as to grudge me this:
not let you live to see my kingdom.
　　—*Aeneid,* translated by Allen Mandelbaum

We are trapped in meanings that circulate like blood.
The sword descends. And He who kills you is not
a myth, nor a city. His eyes searching yours could
be a lover's eyes. It was love He fought.
　　—Rosanna Warren

A miracle, six-month library loans,

equinox to equinox and equilaterals

are my least favorite shape because

equality is a fool's dream. The number sixty,

popular with the Babylonians, but no one

could ever get a good footing on such an incline.

Virgil said stepping into hell was easy,

it was the first step back that tripped you

up, but I'm paraphrasing, lost

in Tiresias's toothy smile right before he downs

a bowl of brackish water, this river

that laughs at time's passage, laughs at you

thinking there is some downed branch

to keep you afloat.

Why not sink below?

Current is still current but at least there's company,

mud-covered rocks and crustaceans to slalom

as you forget the lack of oxygen, sudden onset of hypoxia

forcing your mouth open to breathe, to mime the words

to your mother's favorite Broadway musical,

"I've just met a girl named Maria"

but soon I'll be stabbed in the throat.

Intention and side effects, Helios's cattle—

tasty tonight but watch out for the indigestion,

cramps followed by your eyeballs melting

and perhaps this is partially my fault.

If my translation were better, then

Chryses would walk away from Agamemnon's tent

along the shore of Ilium, dejected, his tears

matching the dark waves rolling in. Instead,

the waves dance instead of roll, this walking staff's a scarf

and everyone complains about the choice of

sandals as footwear in a blizzard.

It's all in how you look at the final word,

& in the *Aeneid* it's *hell*;

such a clamor and clattering in the dust,

so many swords ringing out in their bitter arguments,

shields fallen as bronze blankets to the dead.

How could there be any other choice?

Burn this, Virgil said, and he wasn't pointing

to his bedpan but the stack of vellum, hundreds

of sheep who gave their lives to found Rome;

we who are about to read salute you!

Because what's a masterpiece without hordes of dead,

human or inhuman? Or foam at the crest of a wave,

the corner of our hero's mouth

as he inserts the tab A of his sword into

the slot B of Turnus's breastplate, here,

in this simple pop-up book, the thrust so soundly repeated

each time I open to the proper page.

## Mucius Scaevola

Gird yourself, if you will, for the struggle—
a struggle for your life from hour to hour,
with an armed enemy always at your door.
    —*The Early History of Rome*, translated by
      Aubrey de Sélincourt

One day, at table, while relating the fortitude
of Scaevola, they were terrified at seeing me
start from my seat and hold my hand over a
hot chafing-dish.
    —Jean-Jacques Rousseau


Clusium is a place

you've never heard of.

When you imagine it, consider

the slow melt of all things: snow

on Porsena's forgotten siege; his peace

emissaries long dead, like firstlings curled

in the fire. The trick is not minding the strong

stench, the leathery skin, the flames choked

with eschar. The trick is remembering

we all march into certain death,

armored, still armed with

the fire's cansema, this

hole's brilliant glow.

# Menelaus Takes Up Sculpting

I came here / in my own shape but lost it on the way.
    —Robert Kelly

Personally, I always found a thousand ships
a little excessive.
    —Evie Dunmore

Menelaus only walks the palace grounds

in darkness; each night, he chooses a new statue

as audience for this eulogy. His metronome:

hammer and chisel; the night: water & dust.

# Daedalus

And where his wings were joined, sweet-smelling fluid
Ran hot that once was wax. His naked arms
Whirled into wind; his lips, still calling out
His father's name, were gulfed in the dark sea.
 —*The Metamorphoses,* translated by Horace Gregory

The boy accepted them;
His whole childhood in them, his difference
From the others. The wings
 —George Oppen

Lately, my son has been naming birds:

grackle and whippoorwill, crow;

he does not know what these names mean,

or why they seem right.

Lately, he knows what a whip is,

the calm birds that sit and watch

from the doorstep;

"they accept pain so gracefully," he says.

Lately, grackles sit by his window,

look in with pale yellow eyes,

scrape their feet against stones in the garden

*like air pushed through a broken nose.*

A crow has never come to our garden but

"if I have a soul, something must be looking for it,"

must see it, hidden inside these walls,

even if he doesn't.

Lately, he says, "the crow consumes"
My son has no food but his eyes,
no drink but his breath, left out
each night as an offering.

Lately, he asks me to build him wings,
more brittle and hollow bones, to replace
his hands, his arms,
*so useless in flight.*

He asks me this each morning, begging,
lips pressed against my knees in supplication.
In his clenched fist, a whippoorwill,
struggling, beak bloodying flesh.

"I can get the timber, father,
I can get everything you need," he said,
smiling at the small bird, petting it,
*pulling off feathers by the dozen.*

## [Notes on Variations in Translation: *Trojan Women*]

In one version of the play, Odysseus is visibly upset

about the death of Astyanax: shaking, muttering to himself. But

this is just what you do: your duty; kill the heir, presume

the breadth of retaliation. In another version, Odysseus is unable

to throw the child from the ramparts and so watches

as the now-somehow-fully-grown prince throws himself from the open

arms of his city; walls of his mother. Or

something like that, if I remember correctly. I assume

this disparity, like all disparity, comes as a result of philosophy.

Seneca, in his sad stoic rhetoric, can't wait to jump from

the roof of this war; a final *fuck you* to every so-called hero.

But he, like most of us, is more like the shaken Odysseus, each

choice already made the moment we arrived; the terrible, terrible

silence that morning at the clinic, as I told Eileen, which is not

her real name, this story. *"Does that mean that John*, which is not his

real name, *is Odysseus?"* she said. *"Because he didn't push for this. He never once pushed.*

*Neither did Odysseus,"* I said, *"depending on which translation you read."*

In this manner, time passed, as she waited to be called.

## The Horses of Achilles

*When they saw that Patroclus was slain,*
*who had been so stalwart, and strong, and young,*
*the horses of Achilles began to weep*
    —C. P. Cavafy

*Why love what you will lose?*
*There is nothing else to love.*
    —Louise Glück

the snow has not ceased since it began

and here is white, and here is water

have you seen the way ice hangs off

the dynamite-touched world? There are

the tips of mountains pushed through

ash & spark against the world's anvil

party to grief because of this fool's gift:

two horses whose names few remember

in the mist of their breath; left

the tears have not ceased since they began

reflecting this road to a stifled ocean, lost valley

these poor wretches; why did we give you to

men climbing the slick surface today,

the fog: haloed, fading into

the bodies of pitiable grief, and you might be

something larger: a house painted against hills,

standing patient in the distance, draped

in the midst of sadness like any other noble creature,

             like you, or me

## Polyphemus on Sheep

They took the olive spear, its tip all sharp
and shoved it in his eye. I leaned on top
and twisted it, as when a man drills wood for shipbuilding
    — *The Odyssey*, translated by Emily Wilson

Ulysses is dead
by now he is dead
And how wise was he
who blinded a thing of immortality?
    —Gregory Corso


Once I saw the world, its grass retreating to rocks, its cliffs bare.

Then a man took my eye, told me he was no one, I was nothing

and never again could sit and stare.

# CONFESSIONS

## On Camping

For each person I've said *I love you* to, the lie
was always there but wasn't understood
until some later date.

Dormant, perhaps, some recessive gene that finally
finds a part in this stage production. Sudden context,
like reading the *Iliad* & realizing sure, there's anger,

but before that there's just a lot of camping.
And what strikes me most is the scepter of Apollo
slowly slipping out of Chryses's hands as he loses

everything in the sounding sea; black ships.
Or how he, like any other father, invokes revenge
not as a single stroke but a thousand bites.

Smintheus, the literal *mouse god*, or maybe
just some flea that won't leave
me. You need to understand

there's this particular tree, hemlock or poplar,
at this particular campsite where she told me
all of this, lectured through the long line of her lips

like ships parted and imparted. That *love* was a word
that could be pushed like pumice stone in a glass of water:
light and porous and impossibly afloat.

## On Woodworking

In his deafness, his private
    wood, work-
        shop beneath the stairs,
          beneath

an empty kitchen, my grandfather
        works

his hands, a kind of
    lathe
        for cherry, american
          black that hems      a seam
          in hum & clatter

                      and
when I speak, he turns,
        watches, this slip
        of lips
   as if
          my mouth is a wave
                a body
        of water, perhaps

                more
                or less

                correct.

## On Brigit Pegeen Kelly

This overpass interrupted
      by                                    glass is an ocean, of sorts:

      the frequency of
              belief in nothing or
              nothing but belief

in sound. Silent,
              now "the sea," Stevens said,
              "was not a mask"
*and neither was she.*

You lost her, and
              I never knew what to say. I still don't

                  know what day
I stopped hearing
the rain,
              this ocean of heather:    the tap
                                     tap
                                     tap that kept
time, on a Tuesday together

          in her office,
              perhaps; to talk about
              smoke, or a feather. I tell you

there were hours spent
on a feather. Silent,
              now, struck
              from the sea. When

I'm not sure. Can't
say. But I miss it.     That much
                          I confess. That much

can be heard

above the rest.

## On Leaving

In the corner of the kitchen was my mother, her suitcase
open, coffee mug placed on her pink cardigan. A heart
on the cup, with letters long scratched away saying
nothing of importance. How it's the end of things
we remember, the way porcelain and clay crack
without protection. Her eyes like tin clasps finally snapped
into place. The door open. Screen's pneumatic
cough. How silent the last idling car in the driveway
leaving like air bleeding off, saying nothing at all.

## On Conversations

There was a moment I realized prayer
is just a conversation with who you'd rather be.

In this same way, confession builds a narrative
in what should be a poem. But who

am I to judge? Who am I to hold
your cheek, that jawbone, in a way

that resembles justice or war, because they follow
in sequence like schoolchildren

hopping in each other's snowy footprints.

I am something of an expert on the thing
not said. I excel at the implied expectation, this vast disappointment.

You met me at a strange time
in my life: all relish and old boots; a hat

that never leaves the bookshelf. I wonder
who we're talking to in the night? Do the stars know

they sit like impossible children in the distance? So quiet
except for a twinkle here, thermonuclear explosion

there. Emptiness filled with metallic sounds
and deadly radiation.

But what isn't, you know?

When I was a boy, I prayed on one knee because
I always thought myself a knight: armored,

and armed and long &, of course, cold.

## On Translation

It's dinner. There is a young couple at the table. The man, who thinks himself a translator, says that *logos* is both the word and the phrase, argument and exclamation, subject and direct object. A man, for example, coming upon the sea may say "alone." A woman, for example, just across the way may say "I have come to the sea." A story may be told later in the evening, after the meal is cleared, and the silverware is replaced with silverware, and the dinner wine is replaced by dessert wine, that "a man and a woman have come to the sea." *Alone,* because one man is, and so this man is as well. *Sea,* where another woman stands now, is where she once stood, and this is too much for her, so she leaves this room, this sea. And so only this man and woman are now left. Left with the sea. What they hear in the translation is merely conjunction: the point at which two things intersect; the act of that intersection. *And* so they stand by the sea. *And* the man refills her wine glass. *And* the woman responds by lifting the glass to her lips. *And* the man is sure he has never seen such a lovely thing. *And* the woman is sure that, despite the loneliness of tidal pools, the sea will remain.

## On James Longenbach

The fawn huddled alone in the backyard has nothing to do

with your death. But here we are. Hurt in the too-long grass

below the window which is both bed and breakfast.

What did Democritus say about blue? Or Heraclitus

on Pythagoras believing he was a sardine in a precious life?

I meant *previous*, but let the mistake stand, you'd say, It's a wonder

anything ever gets done, Jim, when the sun only peeks through the ivy-

choked afternoon. It's a wonder white spots can be so

symmetrical on the back of new life, or the end of it, I suppose.

I called animal control. I asked how to save this small thing. I was told

nothing could be done. Nothing. "A movement of language. Small

enough to remembered whole, difficult enough not to be forgotten." I say to the night:

he might be right here, still, in the *wine-looking* dark. But I don't

know. Eventually, even the sun shrugs its way out of view.

## On Woodworking, Again

When my grandmother died, my father bent
       down on his right knee, genuflected to the small toy city before me.

His eyes, like all mirage, shifting: light to dark, red from blue.

Will you bury the beryl sweater, or the long strands
       of yarn that hung from the open drawer of her sewing desk?

Will you cross her hands at the matted folds
       that pressed against you like crumpled paper? How can you

force air into something already filled with blood?

Imagine: the day she was buried, my grandfather
       planted a black oak in our yard. Imagine:

the sapling's branches, as thin as my ring finger. Imagine: how
       long you'd wait for a single leaf, or to peel a piece of bark

with your pocketknife like blistered skin.

"They seldom live more than two hundred years," my grandfather said, showing me
       how to fleck dirt from the roots with my fingers.

*Some things we put down knowing we'll never pick them up again.*

## On Beauty

Once, in a moment of anger, my mother
     asked her son why

         he wasn't happy

that there was a time, she

     remembered

         he was happier
& I heard

               nothing, said
               without thought
               I only wanted

to be beautiful

               I knew

that sadness
was beautiful. If nothing else        she had taught me that.

## On Jake Adam York

When you died, the sun cast off all
its heavy elements. No, it was the son,
and gilded trees cast shadows back
to the river's grin. No, there was no
water or gold or reasons given. There
was only loss, like wordless mouths, or
glass eye placeholders lying in each holy
moment. No, it was stained glass, it was
cochineal and mordant and woad. Every
empty tracery filled, made from the world
boiled down, the world crushed. No, it
was something else, some deep shade of blue,
lit and falling. The late afternoon lost
here, like so many others, when I heard.
What light remained only dark diffused across
my face. No, it wasn't light. It was
something else entirely.

## On Woodworking, One More Time

When he could no longer climb the stairs
my grandfather simply stopped woodworking.

In time, the house forgot this sound.

When he could no longer walk the beach, my father said,

      quietly, as if to the ocean,

        "Take a seat, Dad,"

    and they sat for hours
        on end, unsure of how to get home, what direction

      was next.

This information,
    like most, was communicated

        over long distances;

    how I can't figure out where
        in the conversation to insert this sort
            of anecdote, that sort of laugh.

                How much of our interactions
                were made up

of the *meanwhile*

      its ever-so-slight needle.

From this curious singularity,
      whole reels let out like overcrowded charter boats,

            or the 8 mm my father transferred to digital
             so he could remind himself

                        just how small all of this once was.

# On the Time It Takes to Fire Thirty Rounds from an AR-15

For if I imp my wing on thine,
Affliction shall advance the flight in me.
—George Herbert, "Easter Wings"

One hundred and sixty-five wingbeats from a ruby-throated hummingbird. Nearly six
hundred from that same hummingbird in front of a perched female. Two hundred
and seventy from a ladybug, or thirty less from a monarch butterfly.
Only fifteen from a swallowtail butterfly, loping when compared
to other insects, but it gets the job done. Five hundred and
forty beats from a bumblebee. Almost one thousand
from an ordinary housefly. An incredible
eighteen hundred from a mosquito
creating that ubiquitous buzz,
but glacial compared to a
midge at more than
three thousand
wing
beats or
the ivory-billed
woodpecker, which is
recorded at more than eight beats
per second, so twenty-four, give or take,
per two-point-uncertain-decimal seconds, repeating.
Fifty-one for a bat at dusk, of course, it's dusk here and
the truth is I began writing this poem the last time *this* happened.
And when I say *this*, that unspecific demonstrative pronoun that points so
carelessly at the ladybug crawling along my hand or the butterfly on our porch,
it's because I can't bring myself to say what else *this* stands for. Because it's dusk & night
comes with wings, or cape; simple shroud or sickly pall that seems to swallow all of these things

# NOUNS
# [THAT SHOULD NOT BE]
# IN THE DUAL

# ἄνθροπος [man]

|  | & |  |
| --- | --- | --- |
| the world kills kind boys | & | we bury the bodies inside men |
|  | & |  |
| the world kills kind boys | & | we bury the bodies inside men |
|  | & |  |
| the world kills kind boys | & | we bury the bodies inside men |
|  | & |  |
| the world kills kind boys | & | we bury the bodies inside men |
|  | & |  |
| the world kills kind boys | & | we bury the bodies inside men |
|  | & |  |
| the world kills kind boys | & | we bury the bodies inside men |
|  | & |  |
| the world kills kind boys | & | we bury the bodies inside men |
|  | & |  |
| the world kills kind boys | & | we bury the bodies inside men |
|  | & |  |
| the world kills kind boys | & | we bury the bodies inside men |
|  | & |  |

.

## σάκος [shield]

on this newly fashioned shield,

portent rather than pity

my grandfather said,

bronzed as broken bones, *bodies*

*forget*—every day a holy-water

index finger like

lions that fall upon

them—you can't save anything

not because I could

but because I would have to look,

at the shield's slow patina—green as day

the mouth tries to say: *I am old*

*there are stars tonight, but I do not remember*

the story is wrong-sided, hanging on

strapped arms—*What's the point?*

in pictures, when loss is

left lying in a road—*you never*

fulcrum to pivot pain away from

the center of a field—savage

straight-horned cattle—*you can't save*

the truth: I never wanted children—

find them, by the side of the road

every day, here

spores spilled from the fruitbody

*though my eyes are young, I know*

*I do not recognize*

even one constellation

# ἄκμον [anvil]

accusative, of course—direct object
*threnody*, in the Greek, meek-sounding
loss; smallest piece of the mind's deep blue
sound here, fettered away in a forge—
I admit my fear of this inevitable loss,
*antiphon* song, over and over, refrain's
control—I mourn the *incus*, anvil in
*cudere*, beat or strike, which seems right
in the soupy spring of day—nothing
left like a sparkling bit of flecked lead
some new knotty soot, interrupting the
sea just planted, years away from taking root

of sound's transitive verb—it's a dirge,
*wail song*, or whale song, or some imperfect
soft cleft my grandfather heard nothing of—
he would point to his ear; shake his head
gloss over the long nights of tinnitus
being unable to regain
the vulgar tongue but actually
there's so much I'm struck by: simple plans
left in the ear's spin or dot's spot
dust I'm afraid of—dust like some cusp,
green carpet suburban summer—tree, yes,
but so impossible to take back now

## βότρυες [grapes]

my father was such a radical he believed in
bunch-stem still attached to
pedicel, so oft-left like
helmet crest, horse-hair
the same as any thorn or spine
cut with scissors, washed
white bowl my mother purchased
and it's not, I realize, death
but pain; that the point of rupture becomes
a scar you'll always see,
this veraison, almost bloody

love, like the stiff bother of
grocery-store grapes—or
spinose, or some soldier's
plume, which can be removed
from any other soft red-fleshed fruit—
hand over hand in this bright night
at a school craft fair—
I'm afraid of
what's always opposite the green stem
no matter how bold it is,
against all you have left

## κολεόν [scabbard]

imagine the brief boy
cast from lure—here, in the trees,
stones on the banks of tired rivers—no
sound of partridge, no bones
here on this boy's head, crowned
nothing but the round set to
stick skelp, walnut stock
barrel—he is empty, looking into
what little drowns
again; how it pushes this boy
with straw-lick hair to mock
muzzle; scared to be *nothing*
*nothing nothing nothing*

taught to push lead from steel,
there are targets; tepid
tracking the crushed-whistle throat
hung dry on the barn door—no horns,
only in a moss-top snap-back hat—
chamber, to bolt, to hammer—he is empty—
plated nickel paid for this old whiskey
a canopy of green where lips could glean
in the ear—here: the sky pulls
from some small corner chair
pride's dare, hollow as steel
then *nothing nothing nothing*
*nothing nothing nothing*

## συμβόλον [knucklebone]

           how much of the hand is fist

my father asks—                 for him it's half

what you'd expect—the tape's temper    between splint and split knuckles:

symbol's useless rigor;            the long ride home—

           for the boy with the torn lip,

it's half what you'd expect         bleaching blood off some

ripped jersey—it's a               fist his father's proud of, no

open palm; when slapped          head swaying like a ship's bow,

beneath the bile black             bronzed waves where we find

           there's water here, then

breath and                    breath and

      breath and                breath and

## πλοῖο [ship]

take this moment—

        it's where I keep my heart

no idea where you are now—I've

only once shown you my anger,

like sharp stones beneath

proud birds who still strut; one more thing

        I couldn't talk to you about

our last May together

what I remember was

        Elsinore—

place it in a tide pool—

        what a strange thing to have

never seen a kingfisher,

my own little *Iliad* of black ships

sand situated in skin again—small cuts,

calm in their moody waters—

        that one day

when I punched a hole in

our fucking door—our own

        Trojan War—

## ὀχεύς [strap of a helmet; bolt of a door]

maybe it's too early for glow, slow as
a cloud slung like what a soldier might carry
home—I'll never understand why
my mother, for example, carried
a set of latrine tools, mosquito netting,
a cat that wouldn't leave her side
her infidelities, she carried those
too, like volcanic stones
that which impossibly formed inside
the open mouth of mountains of what
one might choose to take

she left our house one day,
a bolt against a red door, and *never* came back
not once more to gather _____
the May lilacs, vulgar in their epithet,
common gift despite only brief flowers,
simple leaves—I understand—no,
eaves in the armor—house filled with the dead
in spent whorls—there's nothing incandescent about
one March afternoon when my mother left like
she'd created—nothing important
before locking the door

## ἀστήρ [star]

any fight is a kind of
geometry—each hit
silks the cage—a wave—boy,

                              this part of speech,
rainbow sneaks—of course, I say         it's about loss—
*thank you* for falling like

        perfect simile—I
        don't know when               some particular piece

                              broke

but I saw edges                    like fragment's
        tent; this city-boy's hands—     stars:

sound ways to navigate
the seas, though not your life—       they lie

                              in beds of black-
                              pooled percussion—

like wood, like gills called
        dead men's fingers;
        Daphne's flight—         I remember the

light lost in a child-
hood's bedroom:                 closed door where

there are cracks in the floor, how   everything seems to be

quiet—it's always quiet,
now, and light tows this *bright,*    impossibly bright snow, sound

        that settles in my ears—once,    my little star,

               I heard every word you said

# NOUNS
# [THAT CANNOT BE]
# IN THE DUAL

αγλαός

[clear water]

in a

ἄγγος

[pail]

αἰχμή

[spear-point]


in the


ἄμολγός

[darkness]

ἱππόκομος

[horse-hair plume]


or maybe


λόφος

[horse-hair plume]

and summer

θύελλα

[storm-wind],

like

κεωεών

[that hollow between the ribs and hips]

which might be the

ἔαυλος

[bed of a stream]

there's a

δράκων

[snake]

in the

φάμνος

[bush]

[thicket]

how a

# εὐλή

[worm]

[maggot]

falls from the

# ἔλαφός

[deer]

# ἔλκος

[wound]

like

ἐρετμόν

[oar]

into

καπνός

[smoke]

[steam]

a

## κίρκος

[hawk]

of course

like a

## θέειον

[sulphur]

## ἱστίον

[sail]

each feather a

# φύλλον

[leaf]


or

perhaps


# φυτόν

[leaf]


or

perhaps


# πέταλον

[leaf]

to this

ἐρῖνεός

[fig tree]

δάος

[torch]

against the

ἀχλῦς

[mist]

κάνεον

[basket]

of

κέρας

[horn]

born like a

μέλισσα

[bee]

from the

# λάναξ

[chest]

[simple box]

of this

# νομός

[pasture]

last

# φαρέτρη

[quiver]

of the fallen

# νεβρός

[child]

[nestling]

[young of a bird]

[foal of a horse]

or

# τέκνον

[child]

[nestling]

[young of a bird]

[foal of a horse]

made

κρέας

[meat]

by the

ξίφος

[sword]

μῦελός

[marrow]

in the

πτέρνης

[heel]

ὄδους

[tooth]


in the


λέβης

[cauldron]

a single

## κύκλος

[ring]

of

## χρῦσός

[gold]

left like

## κλῆρος

[lot]

[marked pebble]

[piece of wood]

in the

λέχος

[bed]


of


τέφρη

[hot ashes]

πῦρ

[fire]

that was once a

ὤψ

[face]

# NOTES

**THIRTEEN WAYS OF LOOKING WEST**

A version of "Walking the Flood of Fire Trail in Kimberly, OR" appears in print and as an audio recording along with the art of Autumn Frederickson on a new waypoint (installed in Summer 2020) at the end of this eponymous trail.

A version of "Watching *Julius Caesar* at the Oregon Shakespeare Festival in Ashland, OR" first appeared in an online interview with Oregon Literary Arts, March 23, 2018.


**NEW DRAFTS OF CERTAIN STORIES**

A list of texts cited in this section, in order of appearance:

Ovid. *Ovid: The Metamorphoses: A Complete New Version.* Translated by Horace Gregory. New York: Signet, 1960.

Castellanos, Rosario. "Hecuba's Testament." Translated by John Frederick Nims. First published in *The Atlantic,* March 1964.

Marlowe, Christopher. "Hero and Leander." In *Christopher Marlowe: The Complete Poems and Translations.* Edited by Stephen Orgel. London: Penguin Classics, 2007.

Aeschylus. *Agamemnon.* In *Aeschylus I: Orestia: Agamemnon, The Libation Bearers, The Eumenides (The Complete Greek Tragedies).* 2nd ed. Translated by Richmond Lattimore. Chicago: University of Chicago Press, 1969.

Russell, Peter. *Agamemnon in Hades.* Aylesford, Kent: Saint Albert's Press, 1965.

Virgil. *The Aeneid of Virgil.* Translated by Allen Mandelbaum. New York: Bantam Classics, 1981.

Warren, Rosanna. "Turnus ('Aeneid' XII)." *Arion: A Journal of Humanities and the Classics*, 3, no. 2/3 (1995): 174.

Livy. *The Early History of Rome.* Translated by Aubrey de Sélincourt. New York: Penguin Classics, 1980.

Damrosch, Leo. *Jean-Jacques Rousseau: Restless Genius.* Boston: Mariner Books, 2007.

Kelly, Robert. "The Menelaus." In *Gods and Mortals: Modern Poems on Classical Myths*, edited by Nina Kossman, 236. New York: Oxford University Press, 2001.

Dunmore, Evie. *Bringing Down the Duke (A League of Extraordinary Women).* New York: Berkley, 2019.

Oppen, George. "Daedalus: The Dirge." Poetry reading recorded on February 19, 1963, at San Francisco State University. Sound Project, 0:39. https://media .sas.upenn.edu/Pennsound/authors/Oppen/SFSU/Oppen-George_08 _Daedalus-the-Dirge_SFSU_2–19–63.mp3.

Cavafy, C. P. "The Horses of Achilles." In *C. P. Cavafy: Collected Poems Revised Edition.* Translated by Edmund Keeley and Philip Sherrard. Princeton: Princeton University Press, 2020.

Glück, Louise. *The Triumph of Achilles.* New York: Ecco Press, 1985.

Homer. *The Odyssey.* Translated by Emily Wilson. New York: W. W. Norton, 2017.

Corso, Gregory. "Mortal Infliction." In *Gods and Mortals: Modern Poems on Classical Myths*, edited by Nina Kossman, 259. New York: Oxford University Press, 2001.

CONFESSIONS

"On Brigit Kelly" is dedicated to my teacher and mentor Brigit Pegeen Kelly, who passed away in 2016.

"On James Longenbach" is dedicated to Jim Longenbach, a friend in poems and in person, who passed away in 2022.

"On Jake Adam York" is dedicated to Jake Adam York, a friend and the first editor ever to publish one of my poems, who passed away in 2012.

"On the Time It Takes to Fire Thirty Rounds from an AR-15" was written after the Parkland School shooting in February 2018.


## NOUNS [THAT SHOULD NOT BE] IN THE DUAL & NOUNS [THAT CANNOT BE] IN THE DUAL

All the Greek in these sections is taken from former Phillips Academy–Andover Professor of Greek Allen Rogers Benner's 1903 text *Selections from Homer's Iliad*. They appear, unless grammatically impossible, in the nominative case as they would have in the lexicon included in Benner's text.

# ACKNOWLEDGMENTS

Thank you to the editors of the following journals in which some of these poems first appeared (sometimes in earlier versions): *American Poetry Review, Capitalism Nature Socialism, Cincinnati Review, Copper Nickel, Ecotone, Gettysburg Review, Palette Poetry, Passages North, Ploughshares, Poetry, Quarterly West,* and *Southern Review.*

Thank you to Forrest Gander for choosing "βότρυες [grapes]" as the second-place winner of the 2020 Palette Poetry Prize.

This manuscript was completed thanks to the generous support and fellowships from numerous organizations, including Dartmouth College; the Frost Place in Franconia, New Hampshire; the James Merrill House in Stonington, Connecticut; Literary Arts in Portland, Oregon; the National Park Service at the John Day Fossil Beds National Monument in Kimberly, Oregon; the Regional Arts and Cultures Council in Portland, Oregon; and the Willapa Bay AiR in Oysterville, Washington.

Special thanks, as well, to representatives from these organizations including, in respective order: Vievee Francis and Matthew Olzmann at Dartmouth College; Maudelle Driskell, Carlene Gadapee, and Jake Rivers at the Frost Place; everyone at the James Merrill House including Randy Bean, Penny Duckham, Cynthia Elliott, Geoffrey Little, Sibby Lynch, Laura Mathews, Bergin O'Malley, R. Douglass Rice, Joanna Scott, and Willard Spiegelman. Additional thanks for their hospitality to Lynn and Jeff Callahan. Thanks to Andrew Proctor, Amanda Bullock, Jessica Meza-Torres, and Susan Moore at Literary Arts. Endless thanks to Sandra Gladish, former Chief of Interpretation and Education at the John Day Fossil Beds National Monument, for Artist-in-Residence fellowships during the summer of 2018 and fall of 2019, and for all her help navigating the park. Thanks to Ingrid Carlson and everyone at the Portland Regional Arts and Cultures Council. And thank you to Cyndy Hayward and my cohort of friends/artists, including Tsering Yangzom Lama, Kisha Schlegel, Michael Fairchild, Jennifer Paige Cohen, and Cris Beam at the Willapa Bay AiR.

Thank you to my entire writing group in Portland, Oregon, especially Jesse Lichtenstein, David Naimon, Alicia Jo Rabins, Ed Skoog, Chrys Tobey, and Vandoren Wheeler, all of whom were instrumental in refining many of these poems, and all of whom I miss dearly. Infinite thanks to so many of the colleagues I've had over the years who looked at or supported this work in some way, including Anna Keesey, Keya Mitra Lloyd, Darlene Pagán, Daniel Pollack-Pelzner, Sara Pirkle, and Brian Whalen. Infinite thanks to my amazing students in recent years from all over the country, especially my Blount Scholars. All of you and your work inspire me.

A big St. Johns thank you to Matt at 45th Parallel Wines for all the time and the fine West Coast IPAs consumed during the writing process. Thanks to Jordan for a multitude of things, including every version of this book he was kind enough to read. And an important thank you to Eily for both reading and listening to so many of these poems. Thank you for listening, still.

A special thanks to G. C. Waldrep for being the best literary pen pal a poet could have. And for his continued support and keen eye.

This book is dedicated especially to the teachers, mentors, and friends we've lost in recent years. None of these poems would exist without you all.

Thank you to my father for reading all of these books in their various forms and drafts.

And thank you to Elizabeth: for every single suggestion, for her infinite patience in listening to me talk about this project for so many years, and for her company on so many of these excursions. And, of course, for all the rest.